eBook Publishing Power For Entrepreneurs:

Secrets the Gurus Don't Teach You

Robbin Simons

Copyright © 2013-2014 Robbin Simons

All rights reserved.

ISBN: 1500909718

ISBN-13: 978-1500909710

CONTENTS

Introduction — Page i

Chapter 1: WARNING! Why Entrepreneurs MUST Have an eBook Today — Page 1

Chapter 2: The TRUTH About Your Book Publishing Options: Traditional, Self-Publishing, Standard Format eBooks — Page 15

Chapter 3: 8 Ways to Create Your Own eBook FAST! — Page 27

Chapter 4: EASY Ways to Transform a Simple eBook Into a LIST BUILDING MACHINE — Page 43

Chapter 5: STAND OUT Strategies for Creating Titles & Sub-titles — Page 53

Chapter 6: How to Choose the BEST Amazon Category for MAXIMUM Visibility — Page 65

Chapter 7: How to Select POWER Keywords for Your eBook — Page 71

Chapter 8: STRESS-FREE Editing & Proofreading — Page 79

Chapter 9: How to Create an EYE-CATCHING Cover — Page 85

Chapter 10: POWERFUL eBook Promotion Strategies   Page 93

Chapter 11: How to Get 1000's of Readers to Download Your Book in 5 Days   Page 105

Chapter 12: The Next Chapter: Why Your eBook is Your New SECRET WEAPON for Building a WILDLY PROFITABLE Business   Page 115

Closing thoughts…   Page 121

Resources [Bonus Section]   Page 125

In gratitude…   Page 127

One last thing   Page 129

A word about community and friendships   Page 131

Finally…   Page 133

About the author - Robbin Simons   Page 135

-INTRODUCTION-

I'm Pulling Back the Curtain & Sharing the Truth!

Introduction

*I*n this eBook I'm going to share some of the unbelievable truths I've discovered from all my hours, days, weeks, and months of research on the vast amount of training and coaching programs available in the market today relating to the subject of self-publishing, eBooks, and writing "best-sellers" in very short periods of time. You will learn the good, the bad, and the ugly truths I have unearthed while designing my own systems and programs that focus on the entrepreneur author who seeks to easily create and publish their own eBook for the purposes of building their subscriber list and growing their business.

Success is not guaranteed, regardless of what you read or hear from all the gurus out there – that's the truth and that's the reality.

It's a balance between great content and great marketing, more than that – it's a marathon, not a sprint, and it's most definitely a journey not for the faint of heart. I teach long-term business growth strategies, not the quick & dirty, "I'm-gonna-promise-you-a-best-seller-just-to-sell-you-my-programs" stuff. This eBook is about solid strategies for writing a simple eBook that's structured specifically for list building and lead generation. It's about creating a tested and proven system for growing a sustainable business and creating solid revenue - plain and simple.

Something you should know about me is that I'm a HUGE fan of Amazon Kindle Publishing, so a lot of what I'll be covering here in this eBook will reference Amazon, but most of what I'm going to share with you can be used even if you decide to publish with Barnes &

Noble or Apple iBooks too. They really are the big 3 that you'll want to consider working with.

But why do you even need an eBook at all? Great question!

Let me give you an idea of the potential impact and reach eBooks can have for your business. In 2008 – in the US alone, eBooks accounted for 1% of the overall trade book market and 3% in 2009. Then in 2010, that number more than doubled to 8%, and in 2011 it hit 19% and up again to approximately 30% last year in 2012.

This information was provided by the Association of American Publishers, and their prediction is that eBooks will hit about 45% of overall trade book sales for this year in 2013. Those are some pretty compelling statistics, especially if you think about how an eBook that is really OPTIMIZED for building your subscriber list and generating qualified leads can benefit your business.

Most eBooks, for those of you who aren't aware of this, can be read on any electronic device such as your desktop computer, a laptop, smart phone, iPhone, android phone, iPad, or any tablet computer. You don't need to have a Kindle to buy eBooks on Amazon, or a Nook to read eBooks from Barnes & Noble. You only need the app which is free to download from the online retailer's website. This a popular misconception, so I just wanted to put that out there just in case this was something you were not aware of.

There is no other tool that's better at building your list, generating qualified leads, growing your business, and positioning you as an instant expert all at the same time than the eBook. By writing your own book, you have the ability to reach so many more people that are looking for the kind of information and solutions you provide. At the same time, you also have the ability to build your prospective client list and get more subscribers to your eZine or newsletter. This is how you can share your knowledge or your gift with the world and grow your business. How cool is that?

As entrepreneurs, we often spend thousands of dollars in promotions and advertising as we strive to attract people to our work and your eBook, if strategically written and positioned, is the number one thing that you can create to draw people to your website and become a "go-to" trusted source and advisor in your field. Your eBook is the key if you're somebody who wants to make money AND you also want to make a difference.

Here's what I know – maybe you've gone through a life changing experience and come out the other side with an important message to share, right? Well, you've already done the hard part, and now you can leverage it to make more money and a big difference in the lives of others doing what you love.

I'm not here to tell you that you're going to sell a million copies of your eBook. But, what I can tell you is, that if you write it, some people will buy it. Almost every eBook sells some copies. And the more books you write, the more money you'll make.

BUT - is that REALLY your goal?

That's question you need to ask yourself. Be completely honest about the answer. Do you want to have a best seller or do you want more sales leads and more traffic to your website? The cold, hard truth is that, just because you write a book, it does not mean it will be a best seller – no matter what you're told by coaches, consultants, and marketing gurus! No one can promise or guarantee your book will be successful or a best seller.

I'm sure you've seen the all the marketing and you've seen the webinars and heard the tele-seminars that talk about how easy it is to make a ton of cash writing a best-selling eBook. You may even be fortunate enough to have actually written a best-seller. If you have, then congratulations to you! That's an amazing accomplishment.

BUT – This does not ensure people will visit your website and opt-in to your subscriber list. It also does not ensure that you'll get more clients, and it doesn't mean that your business will grow as a result of just writing a book or even having a best-seller.

Prior to discovering how to create list-building, lead-generating eBooks, I was doing my best at marketing my business. I did all the things we're supposed to do to get the word out about my business. I did Facebook Ads, Linked In marketing, I joined networking groups, and all of the things recommended and taught by many experts in the online marketing industry.

But the thing about using those techniques to market my business was that there were so many others running the same kinds of ads for the same kind of services. And, as you may have also experienced, it's tough to gain creditability or become known and stand out as an expert in your field when there are so many other very qualified (and sometimes not so qualified) people out there using the same marketing techniques and competing for the same clients.

I spent thousands of dollars on Facebook ads that got a lot of clicks, and maybe only a few opt-ins to my list, but there were really no solid results or a decent return on my investment. And, if you have ever run Facebook or Linked In ads, or even Google Adwords, you know how it works. Your credit card is charged every time a curious browser clicks on your ad. Many of these "curiosity clickers" have no intention of opting in to your list or signing up for your tele-class or your services or programs. But, you know what? You still get billed for every single click!

Don't get me wrong, Facebook and Linked In ads do work for some people, and I truly hope, if you choose to try this method of marketing your business, it works for you and that you get lots of new leads from all your hard-earned dollars. Unfortunately, I have many clients who share these same experiences prior to working with me and creating their own list-building, lead-generating eBook.

This is why publishing eBooks, especially with Amazon, is so powerful and valuable for speakers, coaches, experts, and entrepreneurs.

As you venture through this eBook, you will come across a few really cool tips that I've unearthed from some of the best marketing and book publishing Gurus in the world today. These *"Great Guru SECRETS"* are highlighted in boxes so you can easily identify and bookmark them for your convenience.

If you're more of a "Cliff Notes" type of person, I completely get it so, I've made life even easier for you by creating the "Guru SECRETS eBook Cheat Sheet" which you can download for free at: www.robbinsimons.com/gurusecrets.

This Guru SECRETS eBook Cheat Sheet includes all the good stuff specifically focused on creating list-building, lead-generating eBooks.

Are you ready to learn a few new tricks about how to easily create your own eBook for list-building, lead-generation and business growth?

OK - let's get started!

CHAPTER 1

WARNING!
Why Entrepreneurs MUST Have an eBook Today

-1-

As a professional speaker, coach, consultant, or entrepreneur, writing a book has become almost as necessary as having a business card or a website. This is because, as a published author, your book provides instant credibility and influence as an expert in your field of specialty.

But writing a traditional book can take months or even years to produce and publish. With electronic retailers or "e-tailers" as they are often called, such as Amazon, Barnes & Noble, and Apple iBookstore, many authors are now turning to self-publishing as an easier and more convenient way to fast-track the publishing of their book..

eBook authoring is the NEW COMPETITIVE ADVANTAGE for today's entrepreneur and is the easiest and the quickest way to build credibility as a speaker or expert.

Expert Recognition

Let's face it. There are droves of people in the world all claiming to be experts in their chosen field of specialty and the competition is fierce, particularly for those hoping to succeed as coaches or consultants. All you need to do is conduct a web search on "life coach", "nutrition or health coach", "small business coach", "career coach", etc. to understand how stiff the competition is.

For example, at the time of this eBook's publication, there are 781,000,000 Google search results for life coach, 650,000,000 Google search results for health coach, and 320,000,000 Google search results for career coach.

However an Amazon search provides 5,583 results for "life coach", 2,505 results for "health coach", 5,852 results for "career coach", and only 327 results for "small business coach".

This data clearly supports the theory that an entrepreneur author, with their own eBook published on Amazon, has a greater opportunity for visibility than by simply taking their chances in the deep sea of Google search results. Think about your own habits when seeking information or resources when faced with a particular challenge. The reality is that Google is generally where people go to search for information, whereas Amazon is where people go to buy.

Creating your own book can open up a vast array of new opportunities for any entrepreneur such as receiving more speaking invitations, the ability to command higher speaking and consulting fees, and can result in requests for media interviews with radio, newspaper, and television too.

Simply put, publishing your own eBook provides social proof and credibility to potential clients. It increases visibility for your brand, establishes your expertise and creates trust because you're presenting your message and your value to the market in a tangible format.

Speaking Opportunities

Published authors are actually more sought after as speakers because they are typically viewed as experts in their field. It is very common for event planners to search Amazon using keywords to identify expert authors when they are in need of a speaker for a function or conference. Your eBook is then able to function as a calling card, advertising your ability and desire to provide such speaking services.

Amazon provides additional promotional power by providing authors with a forum to showcase their biography and other professional works through their Author Pages. This is the perfect place to showcase your biography and provide up-to-date information about yourself and what you do. When setting up your Author Page, you should take full advantage of this space. You will have the opportunity to include photos, videos, events, and you can even connect directly to your blog and social media too!

If it is your goal to increase your number of speaking engagements, then it is advisable that you also ensure your eBook Author Biography and Amazon Author Profile specifically state that you are available for speaking engagements and specific the topics or titles of your key talk topics.

The same holds true for consulting opportunities. As illustrated previously by the comparison of Google and Amazon search results, instant credibility and greater visibility are provided as a result of creating and publishing an eBook on your area of expertise, allowing you to stand out from the crowd of others who may be equally qualified.

So, write and self-publish your own expert eBook, set up an Amazon Author Profile Page and you will likely see an increase in well-paying speaking and consulting opportunities.

No Cost Advertising

As I mentioned earlier, social media advertising on platforms such as such as Facebook and Linked In and search engine ads like Google Adwords, can be very costly.

You're credit card is charged every time a curious browser clicks on your advertisement. Many of these "curiosity clickers" have no intention of opting in to your list or signing up for your tele-class or your services or programs. But you know what? You still pay for every single click.

Self-publishing your own eBook provides a cost effective alternative to traditional and online advertising. Actually, a well constructed, list-building, lead-generating eBook doesn't have to cost you anything at all!

Let's break this down. These are the key elements that go into the creation of an eBook:

- Writing the content: $0.00 (Author provides the content)

- Editing/proofreading: $0.00 (Although not recommended, this can be done by friend, family member. Optionally, this can be done professionally for $200+)

- eCover: $5.00 (I use www.fiverr.com where jobs like this cost only $5.00, however you can also have this done by a graphics designer for about $300)

- File formatting: $0.00 (There are many easy-to-follow guides provided by Amazon that make it simple for you to do the formatting yourself. Alternatively, a professional can do this for you for under $200)

- Uploading to Amazon: $0.00 (There is no cost to set up an Author account or sell your eBook on Amazon – and it's really EASY to upload too!)

Depending on how much involvement you choose to have in self-publishing your eBook, the cost can realistically range from $0 up to $750 or more. The clients I work with tend to have incredible results from spending less than $100 on all the elements combined that I've listed out.

Compare the cost of self-publishing your own eBook with that of online or social media advertising and

I think you'll agree that the savings and the potential for a more than favorable return on your investment is well worth a try! Unfortunately, online Facebook, Linked In, and Google Adwords run on either time or dollar limits. Once your budget runs out for the day or week or month, your ad is taken down until the next day or when you re-enroll. But once published, your eBook continues to live on, telling your story, advertising your products and programs, substantiating your expert credibility, and reaching millions of interested readers all over the world – FOREVER!

List Building

eBooks also create a unique opt-in opportunity when they're structured and formatted specifically for list-building and lead-generation. This can be as simple as including a link within your eBook that brings the reader directly to an opt-in form on your website.

A great way to take full advantage of this strategy is to offer the reader something that is directly related to your topic and provide the link within your eBook. A downloadable template, audio, video, quiz, assessment, or sample chapter from your next eBook are all unique and creative ways to entice your reader over to your website or special landing page where they are required to provide their email address or other contact information to receive your offer.

The trick to this is not being to salesy or blatantly self-promotional within the eBook. Readers will see right through this and it could result in negative reviews being posted about you and your book. Use care when determining the best location and positioning for your opt-in offer.

Global Visibility

Publishing your own eBook creates a mind-blowing, global platform allowing you to touch the lives of more people the instant your eBook is published and available online.

Once you publish your eBook, it will be available to over 3 billion readers in close to 200 countries for instant delivery. Just think of your eBook as a virtual billboard for your business that is working 24 hours a day, 365 days a year, to promote your book and your business to readers looking for the exact information you've published using your experience or knowledge or message that you have shared. Your dream book will be present on all the top eBook retailer shelves, and readers will discover it through online merchandising systems, search engines, reader reviews, and social media. By leveraging technology and platforms like Amazon, your eBook and your business becomes searchable and findable all over the world – FOREVER! Not just until you reach your advertising budget limit for the week and your ad disappears.

So, as you see, each day that your book sits unfinished, you're undoubtedly losing money, speaking opportunities, publicity and the ability to impact more lives. Just think about that for a minute. How much money are you losing every single day your book isn't available? What's stopping you right now? Is it the fear that writing an eBook is too complicated or takes too much time. Or maybe you just don't know where to start? Well, if any of these reasons resonates with you, then that's an easy fix.

CHAPTER 2

The TRUTH About Your Book Publishing Options: Traditional, Self-Publishing, & Standard Format eBooks

-2-

Traditional, Hard or Soft Cover Books

*I*t's easy to become enamored by a book agent's or publishing expert's promise of making your book available in stores. This is dream we all have. Walking through the aisles of Barnes & Noble or Chapters Indigo and finding your own book sitting on the shelf where you can actually pick it up and show it to the unsuspecting shopper next to you, announcing to him or her (and anyone else who happens to be within ear-shot) "I wrote this book you know. I'm a published author!" Not so fast. You'll want to check the fine print on this one, because your book being available in stores does not necessarily mean it will be available on the shelves in stores. Unfortunately, it is more likely to mean your book will actually be made available online for order and pick up in stores.

The thing you need to understand about traditional book publishers is that they expect YOU to do most of the heavy lifting when it comes to marketing your book. This is one of the reasons they give authors book advances – so YOU can use it to market your own books. The really sad thing is, that after all is said and done, an author's royalties typically amount to under $3 per book on a hard copy book that the publisher is selling at $29.95. This is because the publisher needs to deduct the cost of formatting, manufacturing, distribution and of course, they need to take their share of profit too.

But then, and here's the big key here – all of this is only IF they accept your book.

In most cases, publishers require writers to work through an agent whose primary job is to identify the titles that publishers will want to publish. Just to give you an idea of what it's like out there, many top-tier agents accept about one book out of every 5,000 authors they sign on. And publishers still reject many of the books represented by agents as well.

What do you think your chances are of being picked up by an even decent book publisher these days? Unless you have a solid following of thousands of social media followers, have a relative or know someone in the publishing industry, or were involved in a really juicy, head-line making scandal, I would say your chances are slim and none.

Let's just say you are one of the fortunate few and a decent publisher does decide to publish your book. You're going feel incredibly flattered initially, and you'll be racing to announce to the world that your book is being picked up by a real, legitimate publishing house. Your life-long dream of becoming a published author is about to come true!

Hold your horses there, Bucko! There are a few little details you should know before you give up your day job. Most publishers will require that they retain the rights to your book, meaning you no longer own the content.

This is very important for you to know and to consider carefully before signing on the dotted line because it means that you can never use that content from your book that YOU wrote to develop into future info products or programs now or in the future.

For some authors, this may not be an issue. However, for the entrepreneur author, signing away the rights to your content is the same as signing away future revenue streams and it defeats the entire purpose for creating your book in the first place. In most cases, a non-fiction book, written by an entrepreneur author generally contains content from their blog, their consulting or coaching systems or programs, or signature talks. This isn't just the bread and butter of the entrepreneur author – it's also the appetizer, the meat and potatoes, the wine, and the desert. It's your entire livelihood. Additionally, for the entrepreneur author, your book is you business card, a tool for engaging and attracting potential clients all around the world, and your platform for validating your expert reputation all rolled up into one nice, neat little package. Are you willing to sign over one of the most valuable assets of your business that easily?

Self-Publishing Traditional Books

Self-publishing can be a much better option, especially for entrepreneur authors who want to maintain the rights to their intellectual property or content. There is no question that self-publishing has become the method of choice for many first-time authors however, there are also many well-known, best-selling authors who have refused to take no for an answer and went on to self-publish their own books. Here are just a few names you just might recognize:

The Wealthy Barber by David Chilton

Peter Rabbit by Beatrix Potter

What Color is Your Parachute by Richard Nelson Bolles

The Celestine Prophecy by James Redfield

The Joy of Cooking by Irma S. Rombauer

A Time to Kill by John Grisham was even rejected by 15 publishers and 30 agents before he went the self-publishing route and became one of the best-selling authors of this century.

Robert Persig's best-selling book, *Zen and the Art of Motorcycle Maintenance*, was rejected 121 before he published on his own and Jack Canfield's *Chick Soup for the Soul* had a harsh 33 "no's" before he opted to test drive the hottest trend in book production today.

As you can see, you'll be in great company if you decide that self-publishing your book is the right strategy for you and your business. As for eBooks, which we will discuss next, there is a big benefit in having the speed to market available with this method. In most cases, you could theoretically write and print your own hard copy book in a matter of a couple of months, or even weeks if you really pushed it, whereas a traditional publishing house could take more than a year to make your book available in the marketplace.

Pros:

- You have a physical product you can use as a business card,
- You can sell on your website,

- You can give away during a draw at events,

- You can sell from the stage.

Cons:

- Considerable cost to manufacture,

- Many publishers require minimum print runs,

- Once published, you're stuck with it – no revisions if it doesn't sell, or worse, if there are mistakes in the content or formatting,

- You could end up with boxes of unsold books sitting in your dining room,

- B&N, Chapters/Indigo (in Canada), other bricks & mortar stores only carry books from big name publishers on their store shelves so you are left on your own to promote and sell your book. For this you need to be an established authority.

- Getting paid – annually or bi-annually? Amazon Publishing pays author royalties monthly in most cases, about six times more often than the twice-a-year standard in the industry.

Traditional, Standard Format eBooks

Another reason to write your own eBook and self-publish it on Amazon is because it's so EASY. It's basically a turnkey operation. Once you've launched your eBook, Amazon takes over for you from there. They handle the sales, provide their own unique brand of marketing, payment processing, search engine optimization (SEO), customer service, tax collecting, delivery, and if you want hard copy, physical books, they handle that for you too through their CreateSpace company! They do it all.

Now, if you're a non-techie type person like me, you'll love this part.

You see, to self-publish your own eBook on Amazon you don't even need a big, fancy website, you don't need expensive tech staff, you don't need a copywriter, you don't need a shopping cart, and you don't need a merchant account. More than ever before, it is now faster and easier to get your eBook written and online than it is to actually put up a website!

I know that, for myself and for many of the

entrepreneur authors I work with, using eBooks to market our businesses has really enabled us to not only grow our businesses but, more importantly, we've been able to really stabilize our lives too. It's worked for us and it can work for you too. This is really for you if that's what you're ready for. You want to get your knowledge out there all over the world and eBooks really do lift all the barriers.

CHAPTER 3

8 WAYS TO CREATE YOUR OWN EBOOK FAST!

-3-

You may already be out there rocking it with eBooks or special reports you've previously written. You might have your eBook posted on your website as a free opt-in offer. But many entrepreneurs find just getting started to be one of the greatest challenges they face once they set their minds on writing. The one thing you need to decide first is what your goal is. This is where it all begins. This chapter will get us all on the same page (pardon the pun!).

The Basics

If your goal is to simply have an eBook to use on your website as a free gift to visitors for opting in to your newsletter or eZine, then this can easily be done in a just a couple of hours. It's really unbelievable how easy it is to put together a 5-10 page basic eBook or special report to use for this purpose and it's a great way to get your feet wet if you're just launching a new business or just want to try your hand at writing.

All it takes is compiling a few of your previous blog posts, putting it into a word document and saving it as a PDF. It's really that simple. You can then ask your website manager or resident techie-person to post it to your email opt-in provider if you're not so technically inclined and you're good to go.

The real benefit to self-publishing your own eBook comes in using your eBook as a lead generation tool, and posting or selling it online in places like Amazon or Barnes & Noble.

So, where do you start? Very simply, you begin with a great idea, your own expertise, a process you have developed, or even a personal experience. Don't over-think it!

TOP SECRET

Great Guru SECRET: You can maximize your ability to hook your reader by following this simple writing structure that I developed specifically for the purpose of getting the reader to know you, begin to trust you, and come to LOVE you:

1. State the problem the chapter will cover
2. Provide 2-3 solutions to the problem
3. Provide a case study or client example highlighting successful results.

Use What You've Got

By far, the easiest and quickest strategy for creating content for your eBook is to simply re-purpose content you might already have such as your own past blog posts or eZine articles. Many entrepreneur authors have had great success with this method of creating content for their eBook and it's a brilliant way to make use of great content you already have without re-inventing the wheel.

So, how can you be sure you're writing about something your market really wants to read? How can you uncover what your ideal client really desires? You can start by surveying your subscriber list.

Get a Little Help From Your Friends

Since you already have an established relationship with the people on your list, this is a great place to find out what they would like to read and what interests them. Start by creating a simple questionnaire with a free survey tool like Survey Monkey. Next, send out an email to your social media community or subscriber list requesting that they take a few minutes to complete your survey. This is a great opportunity to get the early buzz going about your eBook before you've even started writing it, so be sure to mention your new writing project in the email as well.

Easy Market Research

My favourite strategy, and one of the easiest and most successful ways to find a solid topic and relevant content for your eBook, is to join Facebook groups, Linked In groups, or other social media groups and niche forums where your target audience or ideal clients hang out. Spend some time there, observing the common pains and challenges experienced by these groups and participate in their discussions. It's important to add value to any group forum you belong to. The more you engage with the members, the easier it is to earn their trust and become known as an expert in your area of knowledge. Popping in from time to time just to promote yourself and your products and programs will not create the positioning you want to attain and may result in creating a bad reputation for yourself.

In short, participate in discussions and pose questions. If you're a coach, this is where your listening and observation skills come in and will serve you well, so pay attention to the problems or challenges facing these group members and add value wherever you can.

TOP SECRET ***Great Guru SECRET:*** If you are having difficulty uncovering a few clear and actionable challenges, then just ask. Post a question asking what they most struggle with. This information is pure gold. This is what your ideal clients want to know about and this is the information you can use to create the solution they will buy from you. You can then take that feedback and write a chapter on each challenge or problem.

Easy Content Creation Process

Once you have an idea of the common challenges facing your target audience, the key is then to structure each chapter in such a way that you are stating the problem in clear terms and emphasizing the pains that come along with that problem. The next step is to provide 1-3 solutions for each of those problems. I love to use this formula for writing just about everything.

To summarize this easy content creation process:

- Identify 3-5 problems mentioned by your ideal clients or target readers.

- For each problem, write down 3 solutions to that problem.

Now, you essentially have the base you need for your eBook or even an article. And it's not only useful for this, but you can also use this same formula for writing blog posts, newsletters, and even speeches or presentations.

Each of those problems and solutions can then be broken down individually and be re-purposed as short blog snippets and even better, you can use them as tweets for Twitter and just about any other social forum post.

Let Me Make This Easy For You

As I mentioned, you're going to be able to use this formula across the board for all your writing requirements. If you're more of a visual-type learner, I've put together a template for you to use so you can see exactly what this structure looks like. You can download this from my website at:

www.robbinsimons.com/gurusecrets.

I think you'll find this formatted template quite useful and you can use it over and over again, with every writing project you work on.

Make It a Group Thing

If writing your book feels like a horribly daunting task, there are other methods you could use to get the job done. A popular method is to create a compilation of stories or content from other contributing authors – with their permission of course. This is the "Chicken Soup for the Soul" model for creating books otherwise know as an "anthology" book. It's a great method, but just be sure there is agreement from all the participating authors on how the book is to be produced, sold, marketed, and how any commissions are to divided and distributed. In this particular situation, it is essential to have a contract in place with all the contributing authors.

Get Others to Write for You

If you really hate writing, you may want to consider hiring a ghostwriter. There's no shame in having someone else write you eBook for you. In fact, this is a very common strategy used by many busy entrepreneur authors. I think you would be surprised by the number of books currently selling on virtual book shelves everywhere that were not actually written by the person listed on the cover. The fact is, not everyone finds writing enjoyable and not everyone is good at it either.

That's why there are contractors and freelancers in the world! So, where do we find them? There are many qualified writers who would love to work with you to create your eBook. You can find them through Craig's List or eLance.com, but my personal favourite is O-desk. Regardless of where you choose to search for your contractor, I recommend that you start by posting just small job for a blog post at first. You can then review the submissions and select a shortlist of candidates to write a larger article, and make your final choice from there.

I love O-desk because you can set a weekly budget for your job that the contractor cannot exceed, which can help you manage the budget you have set for your project. They also provide screen shots of your project as it progresses so you can see the work being accomplished along the way.

And here's little tip - be sure to look at their O-desk English scores to be sure you are hiring someone that has the language competency you require for your project.

If you still find yourself stuck and staring at a blank computer screen, I would be happy to help you get clear, find your way and get back on track. My 2-hour power strategy session was designed specifically for this purpose if ever you find yourself in this position or if you would like help understanding where and how your dream book can fit into your business. The details are on my website at www.robbinsimons.com/starthere. Did you notice how I just made you an offer and provided you with the link back to my website to find out more information?

Talk It Out

Another super simple strategy for writing your eBook is to transcribe yourself talking on audio. I love this method and I use it in many of my Entrepreneur Author workshops.

This is how it works:

- Create an outline of what you want to cover in your eBook.

- Record yourself speaking about each of the points in your outline.

- Transcribe the audio yourself, or hire a transcribing service to do this work for you.

- Viola' – you have an instant eBook ready to go!

Choosing a topic for your book is a lot like choosing a business idea. Sometimes you choose it and sometime it chooses you.

Here's a really cool thing about eBooks - with traditional publishing, if your book doesn't sell, the publisher sends all the books back to you. With ePublishing, if your book doesn't sell, you can re-purpose your original content, re-title it, maybe even put a fresh, new cover on it and try it again, all without any additional, significant investment other than a couple of hours of your time.

What I'm getting at here is, don't stress over this too much. Write what you know. It's really just that simple.

CHAPTER 4

EASY WAYS TO TRANSFORM A SIMPLE EBOOK INTO A LIST BUILDING MACHINE

-4-

Before we go on, just let me make it clear that I have no affiliation with Kindle Direct Publishing or Amazon or any other publishing platform. I think by now you can understand why eBooks are such a great way to market and grow your business. But, I want to share a secret with you.

There are many author coaches out there that will help you write your book in a weekend or host your book on their websites for you with the promise of greater visibility, greater sales, and even best seller status. What they don't get (maybe they do get it, but they surely aren't sharing this secret with their clients) is that if strategically prepared, published, and promoted, your eBook can actually generate thousands of fresh, new leads for you every single month. That's the difference between writing and creating a typical, everyday eBook versus a list-building, lead-generation eBook.

That may sound like typical, over exaggerated, marketing-speak but it is the honest truth – no BS.

Goals

The first step in determining the best structure for your eBook is coming to terms with the true purpose of your eBook – what are you trying to accomplish? Is it your goal to gain visibility and grow your business, or is it to fulfill your fantasy or burning desire to become a published author?

Look inside yourself first and decide what your goal is for your eBook. Is it to make a couple of hundred dollars a month in extra cash, or is it to use your eBook as a list-building, lead generation tool for driving traffic to your website. Or maybe it's all of these things!

Decide the reason for writing your eBook and write your book with that reason and goal in mind from the beginning.

The way you construct your eBook obviously has a direct correlation to how you will entice your readers back to your website. This is the primary purpose of a list-building, lead-generation eBook and should be your ultimate goal. Move them back to you home turf.

Standard Structure

The standard length for a non-fiction eBook is approximately 20,000 - 30,000 words and around 80,000 words or more for fiction eBooks. But, there is no reason you can't publish a smaller project such as a booklet, pamphlet, or brochure with only about 15,000 to 20,000 words. It's all about providing great content, and if you can do that with fewer words and in a smaller format, then go for it!

A past coaching client of mine, a holistic nutritionist, experienced enormous success a result of publishing a series of short pamphlets on varying dietary options.

Each pamphlet addressed a specific type of dietary option such as vegan, Paleo, low carbohydrate, low fat, etc. and each followed the same format providing an overview of the diet, pro's and con's, sample menus, and shopping guide.

The strategy we developed was actually quite brilliant, and one I use often if the entrepreneur author provides a service or program. We first developed a marketing and promotional calendar fro my client's business and then positioned regular releases of each eBook in her series. This created a buzz about her business and events and enabled her to successfully build her email list prior to promoting her new coaching programs. She released a new pamphlet each month for 6 months, aligning each release with the promotion of a new coaching program.

Regardless of the amount of content you choose, your eBook should always include:

- A title page that includes the book's title, author name's, and website

- A copyright page that states the copyright and disclaimer page, just like you would include on your website

- Table of contents – It's important NOT to put page numbers here because eBook readers or tablets will change the page numbers depending on their format or the size of font the reader chooses. Just identify the chapters and sub-chapters but do not include the page numbers.

Table of Contents

It's important to understand that your Table of Contents must contain information that is crystal clear and compelling. Your Table of Contents is the best tool you can use to persuade an undecided reader to buy your eBook. This is where the reader instinctively goes to decide if your book is worth buying so it's important that your chapter titles are clear and specific to the actual content. Name your chapters in a way that the reader will know exactly what they're getting and stay away for the cutesy, ambiguous chapter names.

Don't Include

It is equally important to understand what NOT to include in your eBook. I advise my entrepreneur author clients to avoid unnecessary or complex formatting. This will only make it more difficult to convert from MS Word format to an acceptable eBook format and will frustrate you beyond belief. It may also cause your eBook conversion to fail, so if you're a rookie eBook author, just keep it simple.

I know many of you aren't going to like this, but try to avoid using too many images throughout your eBook as well. Pictures are great and I know it's nice to add visuals to books to break up all the text, but this can add to the file size and you may be charged additional electronic delivery fees if you exceed the maximum file size limit. I believe the current file size limit for Amazon is 25 MB at this time, but you'll want to check this each time you go to upload a book to be sure the limits haven't changed. Ultimately, you may need to decide if it's worth it for you to include images in your eBook. The secret to eBook formatting is just to keep it simple.

Great Guru SECRET: If you want to include a diagram, a template, a picture, or other image that is relevant to the content or message of your eBook and beneficial for the reader to have, then this is the perfect opportunity to replace the image with a link from your eBook directly to your website where the reader can go to opt-in and receive the diagram or template, or even a video instead. Now, that WOULD be cool!

CHAPTER 5

STAND OUT STRATEGIES FOR CREATING TITLES & SUB-TITLES

-5-

*F*iction and non-fiction books should really be titled differently. Non-fiction titles should be longer, include subtitles, and should include relevant keywords in both the title and sub-title, if at all possible.

Remember that your title is the first thing a potential reader will see before deciding to read or buy your eBook. It's important to understand that people don't read – they scan. So, if you're to trying catch the attention of the online book browser, you surely don't want to make them work too hard to figure out the meaning of your book title, because they won't. Potential readers simply will not take the time so it's important to create a clear title that is instantly understandable yet compelling at the same time. This is much easier to do with a non-fiction eBook as long as you don't get caught up in trying to create cute or overly creative titles.

The formula for creating a clear and compelling title is relatively simple. Begin with the short title, or your headline title, which tells the reader what the book is about then add a longer sub-title that explains the benefits.

Here's an example:

e-Book title or headline title is: The Holistic Health & Wellness Entrepreneur's Essential Handbook for Success

Subtitle: Easy Ways to Make More Money Doing What You Love

Do you see how that works? The headline title tells you exactly what the book is – it's a handbook written for health & wellness entrepreneurs and it's essential for their success. And the sub-title clearly explains the benefits the reader can expect as a result of buying and reading this book – they will learn how to make more money doing what they love.

You can understand why it's important to create clear titles that tell the reader who the book is for and why they should buy your eBook over any another eBook.

Why does all of this matter? The title you choose for your non-fiction book plays a "make or break" role in its success. By choosing the right title, you can establish an instant connection with your potential readers. The right title clearly indicates who should buy your book, why they should buy it, and how they will benefit from your eBook. But, if you choose the wrong title, your book essentially disappears into the abyss. Just as the headline is the most important part of an advertisement, the title is really the promise that attracts readers (and search engines) to your eBook and engages their interest.

To construct a solid title for your eBook you'll want make an obvious promise. Choose a title that clearly describes the change your book will help readers enjoy. Readers buy non-fiction books for a purpose.

The best titles promise to solve a problem or help readers achieve a desired goal.

Compare the following two titles:

Organic Gardening Tools & Techniques

Healthy Earth, Healthy Food, Healthy Body: A Guide to Organic Vegetable Gardening

Which do you think sold best, and continues to sell? Hint: the first title simply tells what the book is all about. The second title emphasizes the benefits that readers will enjoy. You'll also notice some great key word phrases that were used too.

Another strategy for creating your eBook title is to identify your ideal readers in your book's title. Prospects will want to read your book because it sounds like it was written specifically for them. This strategy enables you to target your market by naming them, or describing their characteristics. Either way, the more obvious you are, the clearer it is to your target reader.

You can also identify your market by describing the circumstances they're experiencing, i.e. *Cooking for Two*.

Be as specific as possible. Try using numbers to add credibility and urgency to your titles.

The use numbers provides structure for your information, as in Steven Covey's *The 7 Habits of Highly Effective Individuals*. With this type of book, once you've identified the secrets, keys, or steps, your book is well on its way to completion.

Numbers can also make big goals appear easy to achieve, by breaking them into a series of easy-to-accomplish tasks, like *6 Steps to Take Your Marriage from Good to Great*.

You can also use numbers to emphasize how quickly readers can get the change they're looking for. For example, when numbers communicate a timetable for success, as in *6 Weeks to Sleeveless and Sexy,* by JJ Virgin.

It's always best to differentiate your eBook from the competition. Non-fiction book titles should position your eBook, or set it apart from other eBooks competing for buyers in your categories. You can set your eBook apart from its competition by emphasizing:

- The people you wrote your book for,

- The challenges your book addresses,

- What qualifies you to write the book and why you wrote it,

- The process or technique you use to solve the problem or achieve the goal

One of the best examples of great book positioning is the *"For Dummies"* series. You know immediately whom the book is for simply by looking at the title.

Engaging your reader's curiosity can also be a really effective way to title your book.

Curiosity can be created by using unexpected words or even contradictory terms to add interest to your book and help set it apart from more boring books on the same topic. A great example of an enticing title that would make you wonder, "what could he possibly mean?" is Keith Ferrazzi's book, *Never Eat Alone*.

Using a metaphor can make titles easier to understand and more memorable. Metaphors make it easy for readers to "picture" what you're talking about. An example of a great metaphor-based title is the *Chicken Soup for the* … series. And of course, Chicken Soup is a metaphor for relief from pain, and makes you think of your mom or grandmother making you feel better when you're not feeling well. You get that warm, comfort food, kind of nurturing feeling from the titles of the books in this series.

Be as clear and concise as possible. Conciseness leads to impact. Think of your eBook's cover as a billboard alongside a busy highway. By using fewer words, a larger type size can be set in the eCover, providing a stronger impact and first impression. Use the minimum number of words needed to explain what your book is about for example *Content Strategy for the Web*. Nothing more is needed. Combine a short title with a longer subtitle that provides additional details.

Here's a really good example of combining a short title with a longer sub-title: *Skinny Bitch: A No-Nonsense Guide for Savvy Girls Who Want to Stop Eating Crap and Start Looking Fabulous.* I love that one!

Keep in mind that you need to create your title in a way your market or your ideal reader speaks. Simply state your eBook's promise in words your readers will immediately understand. Readers should be able to understand your eBook's promise at a glance, like Michael Port's best-seller, *Book Yourself Solid*. Non-fiction book titles can never be too simple or too obvious.

While there are no universal "formulas" for nonfiction book title success, there are techniques and tools you can use, like surveys, to improve your chances of choosing the right nonfiction book title.

TOP SECRET

Great Guru SECRET: When you start to get serious about a title, see if the website URL is available. Register it as soon as possible. If the exact title isn't available, try adding words like "Online," or "Book" to the end of URL.

CHAPTER 6

HOW TO CHOOSE THE BEST AMAZON CATEGORY FOR MAXIMUM VISIBILITY

-6-

Choose 2 BROAD categories – there are 31 broad categories in Amazon's non-fiction listing. Choose 2 broad categories and 1 sub-category. Optimize your sales by category jumping.

How great would it be if Amazon promoted your eBook for you at no cost? This is what happens when you hit the top ranks in your category. That's why choosing the RIGHT categories to list you book in is so important. Amazon's algorithms keep a close watch your sales statistics and, if your eBook is doing reasonably well, they pick up on the fact and reward you. Consistent sales and downloads can indicate that you're content legitimate and sought after, and their customers obviously want your book. As a result, Amazon is going to reward you and give you more visibility by showing your eBook in the section called "Customers Who Bought This Item Also Bought".

Before you know it, Amazon is promoting your eBook for you and you've become positioned on the same sales page as other best-selling books in your genre or category. It's like you're eBook and your business are being displayed on a billboard right in front of your competitor's store.

Choosing the best category for your eBook is not as complicated as you might think. Amazon allows you to list your eBook in two categories. You can start by looking up other books similar to yours or have complimentary. Take note of which categories these book are listed in. A popular strategy used by many eBook authors is to choose one category that you can easily rank well in and another category that will give you exposure to more readers. The key is to find at least one category that fits your eBook and has fewer titles listed than some of the more competitive categories.

Although you can list you eBook in only 2 categories, you have the opportunity to be added to more categories by using tags. A tag serves as a label for your eBook and is relative to the content, the style, or any other aspect of the text. You can tag your eBook yourself through Kindle Direct Publishing, but your readers can also tag your publication as well. If readers tag your eBook with a common key word, you could even find that Amazon could automatically include your it in multiple categories, giving you even more visibility on their site.

CHAPTER 7

HOW TO SELECT POWER KEYWORDS FOR YOUR EBOOK

-7-

Because Amazon is considered to be a highly powerful search engine, choosing the right key words will help people find your eBook more easily during searches. You can list only 7 key words for your eBook, so you'll want to choose these words carefully and enter the most important key words first. If possible, include key words in your title and/or your subtitle, but do not sacrifice the integrity of your title for keywords.

You can also enhance the search engine optimization (SEO) for your eBook by including keywords in your chapter titles where it's often much easier to include than in your keywords in the title or subtitle.

Another great strategy that helps to optimize your Amazon platform is to include keywords in your eBook's description on your Amazon sales page. A good rule of thumb is to aim for 3-5% keyword inclusion throughout the description on your eBook's Amazon sales page.

If your eBook description is about 500-700 words, then that would mean you could include about 35 keywords or keyword phrases in your description. In general, you should choose words that relate specifically to your eBook but are also general enough to attract readers looking for a broad category of information.

Nonfiction books should include keywords related to your topic, your ideal client or target audience, the problems that you tackle, the challenges faced by your target reader or ideal client, or your area of expertise. Choosing the right keywords is really balance between the number of people searching for a particular keyword and the competition for that keyword.

The best strategy to understand this balance is utilizing keyword research tools that can help you discover how people are actually searching the web. By understanding how people are searching for your product or service, and how much competition you have, you'll have a better idea of which keywords to choose to accomplish your goals.

To start with, a creative and effective way to determine your key words is to think of what someone would type into Google if they were looking for your product or service. If you're not sure, then ask someone. This is actually a great question to ask on your survey, which we talked about in a previous chapter. Once you have a few words in mind, you can then research these keywords using a keyword research tool. There are some good free tools available on the web like Keyword Spy and Google Adwords. These tools can tell us which keywords have the greatest potential for ranking in the search engines.

Another little-know secret to selecting key words and phrases is AMAZON. As I've mentioned many times, Amazon is one of the largest search engines on the planet, competing with the likes of Google and You Tube, of course. The really cool thing about this is that nearly everyone who visits the Amazon website is a buyer! So, a great place to start to identify your key words and phrases is Amazon's own search bar. Typing in a key word for your book will produce a list of the most entered search terms or phrases that book buyers are searching on for books similar to yours to actually purchase. Here, you can find the most common phrases that buyers are using to search for books they are interested in purchasing. Play around and experiment with Amazon's search bar by typing in different words and phrases that appeal to you to see what types of books actually come up in the search.

A simpler way of approaching the selection of the best keywords for your eBook is to use exactly the same process you would have used when choosing keywords for your website. Making the right keyword selection is a balance between the number of people searching for a particular keyword and the competition for that keyword.

Here's a word of warning about key word search. Higher search word results aren't always better. It's important to understand that there are no hard-set rules to choosing your keywords. When you look at the results from your keyword selector tools, you will want to weigh the number of searches for a keyword against the competition you might get for that keyword.

If a keyword has 100,000 monthly searches, the competition for that keyword is probably strong, and the chance of your eBook ranking for it are a lot smaller than a keyword that is much more specific to your topic and may only have a couple hundred to a few thousand searches monthly. There's nothing worse than creating an eBook description with a focus on specific keywords only to discover no one's searching for that keyword.

Where possible, try to create opportunities throughout your eBook to include keywords and keyword phrases. You can start by identifying your top 12-15 keyword phrases, then re-read your eBook and look for some generic content that you could easily replace with one of these keyword phrases.

Be sure that you're creating opportunities to use your keyword phrases in a way that feels natural and not blatantly promotional. And don't use the same keyword phrase more than three times otherwise your eBook will begin to sound repetitive and generic, and not to mention annoying!

CHAPTER 8

STRESS-FREE EDITING & PROOFREADING

-8-

The first thing you should do once you've completed the first draft of your eBook is to put it away for a week or two, and take a break before re-reading it. Many authors can't see their own spelling or grammatical mistakes no matter how closely or carefully they read their books and sometimes it is just much easier and safer to have someone else proofread your eBook for you. So here are a few tips to help you proof your eBook:

- Swap with other authors in the forum.

- Ask for a volunteer from your list.

- Hire a freelancer from eLance.com or odesk.com.

- Ensure your eBook flows from chapter to chapter. Are any chapters missing, does anything seem out of place, redundant, or repetitive?

- Are all the chapters in the right order?

- Keep your paragraphs short and clear.

- Fix any confusing or awkward sentences – read your book out loud.

- If you're stumbling through a sentence, it's probably something you should re-write, so try breaking it into 2 shorter sentences.

- Consider using bullet points or lists if you have a paragraph that discusses several points. They're easier for the reader to absorb and can add visual interest and white space to the page.

- Cut out unnecessary or filler words. Some of the most common filler words are "really", "very", "mostly", "usually", or phrases like "in my opinion", "I think" and "I believe".

- Spell-check VERY CAREFULLY and watch for those pesky synonyms like "their, there, and they're".

- Don't rely too much on spell-check. It does not always catch words that are used out of context. Many words won't be caught because you may have typed a legitimate word or phrase, even if it isn't what you intended.

- A good editor can make all the difference in your finished eBook, so consider investing a little extra time and a few dollars in a qualified book editor before publishing.

CHAPTER 9

HOW TO CREATE AN EYE CATCHING ECOVER

-9-

Your book's eCover is going to appear in the Kindle eReader or reading app on the reader's computer or other electronic device, however it will only appear in a thumbnail size, which is basically the size of a postage stamp. It will also appear on your eBook's Amazon sales page or landing page so it is important to make your eCover stand out so it can be easy to read in both color and black & white. Most importantly, ensure the title can be read easily and clearly at a glance. The subtitle is not quite as important so, if you have to make sacrifices, that would be the place to make them.

Crisp images, clear fonts, and bold, primary colors will draw the most attention at a glance but, by all means, use colors that are appropriate to your eBook's content. For example, if your eBook is about holistic healing, choose colors that are soft and soothing like aqua blue, lavender purple, white, or something similar. The use of black or grey or even red, in this case will cause your eBook to lose its appeal to your ideal readers and may not align with the message or experience you're trying to convey.

Color increases a readers' attention span by 82% and makes an impression that is 39% more memorable, so go ahead and be bold, and don't be afraid to use color. It is essential that your title be as legible as possible at varying resolutions. Strong, contrasting colors are likely to have the most impact and be the most readable and highly noticed. The point here is that color appeals to the senses and can convey a message, so be selective with your cover choices.

It's also important to be unique and to stand out. If you are choosing the images yourself, select ones that are distinctive and original, as well as appealing.

Take a look around Amazon or other online book retailers and check out all of the other eCovers in your categories, then design your eCover in a way that is unique and stands out from the crowd.

Focus on one theme and don't over-clutter your cover. Think about the driving message of the eBook and use this as inspiration for the design. Online eBook retailers will likely display your eBook cover as an 80 x 115 pixel thumbnail, so it's important that your cover design is clear and readable at different resolutions. By viewing your draft eCover image at varying image sizes you can ensure it is eye catching, even in a small, thumbnail size. The optimal size for obtaining the best quality for your eBook cover is 1563 pixels x 2500 pixels.

A couple of great resources for getting your eCover designed are: www.fiverr.com and www.99designs.com With Fiverr, you can contract a graphic artist to design an eCover for you for only $5. Be sure to review samples of the artist's work to make sure it feels like a fit. But for 5 bucks each, you could probably afford to pick 3 or 4 artists that have some good samples and get each of them to provide an eCover for you. Then you can choose the one you like best, or better yet, let your community choose it for you!

I like www.99designs.com as well. This site is wonderful because you're able to have a whole bunch of graphic designers produce an e-Cover for you, then you just select the one you like. You begin by posting the job, stating any requirements you may have like color preferences, title, subtitle, etc., then all the interested artists provide their samples that you get to choose from. The payment then goes to your selected artist. It's a little pricier, but it is well worth the investment.

To avoid looking unprofessional and amateurish, it's a good idea to avoid using standard clip art or too many images on your cover. This can create an impression that you are lazy and just threw your cover together which, to the reader, could also indicate that the content was created in the same way. And never use any image without permission from the owner or designer. One simple, unique image on the cover will go a long way in creating a clean and attractive impression that will catch the reader's attention. Additionally, too much text can be a distraction to a book browser, so a good design tactic is to use easy to read fonts that will display well in both a thumb nail size and the standard size on your eBook's sales page.

One last tip: Avoid using the word "by" in front of your name. This is a telltale sign of an amateur author.

TOP SECRET

Great Guru SECRET: Get your community, friends, and fans engaged in your eBook creation project by having a few sample covers designed and post them on your Facebook and Pinterest profiles. Ask your followers to vote on their favorite by sharing, liking, or commenting. This is a fantastic action you can take to create a viral effect for your eBook before it even launches! (but we're going to talk more about this in another chapter)

CHAPTER 10

POWERFUL EBOOK PROMOTION STRATEGIES

-10-

Although I wanted this eBook to primarily focus on creating a list-building, lead-generation eBook I also want to give your some ideas for promoting your eBook, so I'm going to give you some really easy-to-implement tips in this chapter.

My next eBook will be full of more advanced eBook marketing and promotional strategies where I'll be going deeper into really promoting the heck out your eBook in ways that will get you even more attention and greater visibility, so watch for this to be published soon.

The thing that many authors, especially entrepreneur authors, don't realize is that the marketing of your eBook really begins before you even start writing your book. Whether you like it or not, you are not only an author, but a publisher author is a marketer as well. As a matter of fact, when it comes to list building, lead generation eBooks, great marketing is actually more important than the content of the eBook itself.

A super-simple, quick win you can implement immediately in under 2 minutes is to update your email signature block. Before you begin writing your eBook you can include– "Author of an upcoming eBook about (blank) or "Author of the upcoming eBook "(blank)" to be released in the spring of 2014.

Another easily implemented tactic is to advantage of prime real estate you already own by utilizing the space on the back of your business card to include your book titles, links, or even QR codes.

On Your Website:

Set up a place on your website to describe or talk about your new writing project. This could be a separate page on your site or you could simply utilize your blog to provide occasional updates about your progress.

You can even include an opt-in for people who would like to be notified when your book has been released and is available for sale.

Once your eBook has actually been released, you can create a hyperlink to send people to your Amazon eBook sales page and your Author Page. Make it as easy as possible for your community to gain access to your eBook at all times.

Get the Word Out

Before you push the "publish" button, send out some free copies to a select group of readers in your community and mention that you appreciate if their would take a few minutes to provide an honest review about your new eBook. By sending an advanced copy of your eBook to people you trust, you are leveraging the time it takes to have the eBook file converted from MS Word to the ePub format by giving your friends the time to read your eBook and prepare their honest review in advance of your eBook being available to the public. Once it is available for public access, your advance readers can quickly go to your Amazon eBook sales page and post their review, providing social proof to new book browsers who are seeking credibility and recommendations for purchasing your eBook. To gain even more visibility, send free advanced copies to some of the influential bloggers in your area of expertise. Just be sure the bloggers you choose are relevant to the topic of your eBook and your target audience.

Include several positive reviews in the front section of your eBook, so when people download a sample or "Look Inside", they can see social proof that they are buying an eBook that comes highly recommended.

Amazon does not allow authors to create a sales page before your book launch, however you can definitely take some time to prepare your eBook description in a way that grabs your reader's attention and entices them to want to buy – and make sure there are no typos! Nothing says unprofessional amateur than a sales page with typos.

Blogs

In the weeks leading up to the release of your eBook, take some time to post a few blog articles about your eBook creation project and provide frequent updates on your website with news about the official launch of your new eBook as well.

For even more visibility and promotional power, you might consider posting the details of your upcoming new eBook in forums like Kindleboards.com and Goodreads.com. There are a vast amount of forums and free download sites you can utilize to promote your eBook. The key to successful promotion in these forums depends on selecting the most appropriate forum for your eBook genre or topic. For example, promoting a "how-to" eBook on buying and selling real estate in California will likely fall flat in a forum that features romance novels. I think you get the point. Choose your venues for running eBook promotions with the same investigation and discernment you would when selecting keywords. Go with what's appropriate for your eBook and select forums where your target audience can be found.

As I just mentioned, providing your community with frequent updates on your blog is one promotional opportunity that's fairly easy to manage, but you should also seek out opportunities to write a guest column for other blogs. Many entrepreneurs and bloggers often welcome the chance to have a day off from their own writing responsibilities, so if you were to approach someone who has a community of your ideal readers, then you have nothing to lose by making contact and offering a simple, pre-written blog post highlighting or reviewing your new eBook in a non-salesy format. What's the worst thing that can happen? They say "no thanks"? If this happens, it's ok.

You'll just move on to the next blogger. Even if they aren't accommodating right now, at least you've made contact, now they know your name, and next time they may just be the one contacting you!

Social Media

Social media enables instant, real-time updates on anything you put out into the world, and your profiles can provide a quick and easy way to promote your eBook at all phases of the creation and launch process. A couple of strategies you can use to promote your eBook in your social media profiles are:

Let people know when your book will be released by creating a count down clock or even just simply stating "Only 10 days to the launch of my new eBook titled xxxx!"

To establish yourself as an expert, update all of your social media profiles by including the title of your new eBook with your name. For example, you could write *"Jane Smith, published author of "Book Title"*. Now you can see why choosing a clear title for your book is so important.

You can automate your Twitter activity by pre-scheduling around-the-clock tweets with links to your eBook's sale page, hitting all the time zones. Using hash tags like #Kindle and #Amazon will create added value and a little boost to your posts. Don't forget to pre-schedule posts to Linked in and Facebook too.

If you publish your own eZine or newsletter, remember to include information about the release date your new upcoming eBook. You could even include excerpts, quotes, or a sample chapter, as well, through email blasts using auto responders.

You can significantly reduce your stress and your time spent marketing your eBook by automating your promotions as much as possible. This strategy will also enable you to actually bask in the joy of your actual eBook launch. Nothing says "Done!" like enjoying a nice glass of wine, reading the social media buzz about your new eBook, seeing your Amazon eBook downloads increase by the hour, and my favorite part, watching your subscriber list grow practically overnight.

This is a time you want to really enjoy. Hey, you worked really hard on this eBook, so this is YOUR TIME – and you should really savor as much of it if as you can.

Tell everyone you know – friends, family, your business network, your community, your subscriber list, the grocery store check-out person, the bus driver, your hairdresser, manicurist, the parents at your kids social or sporting activities – everyone!

A wise mentor once told me to tell 3 people per day what you do in your business – this also goes for promoting your eBooks! *(Thanks Joy!)*

And by the way, one of really great benefits of putting these strategies in place BEFORE your start writing your eBook is that you'll be creating your own sense of accountability for actually COMPLETING your book. This is the piece I see so many great authors, experts, and entrepreneurs struggle with. It's getting over the finish line. You'll have no choice but to complete and publish your eBook because you'll be shouting it out to everyone and putting it out there for the whole world to see that you are about to become a PUBLISHED AUTHOR! Now, how great is that?

Great Guru SECRET: When doing any promotion, its important to educate your audience about how eBooks and Kindle work and that you do not need to have a kindle device to purchase or read your eBook. Help followers become part of the Kindle experience even if hey do not own a Kindle by providing easy access to download apps required by other devices such as Android phones, iPhones, Nook devices, and others.

CHAPTER 11

HOW TO GET 1000'S OF READERS TO DOWNLOAD YOUR EBOOK IN ONLY 5 DAYS!

-11-

Throughout this entire publication, you've learned a lot about eBooks - how to write them, how to structure them, and how to promote them. Now that we're coming to the end of road, I want to share with you the real POWER behind writing your own list building, lead-generating eBook. This power is the ability to drive people to your website and get them to opt-in to your list. By creating your own eBook and publishing it on Amazon, you will have the power to share your message with the world and grow your business, all at the same time.

Amazon's Kindle Select Program

Amazon's Kindle Select Program allows you to give away your book up for up to 5 days every 90 days. If done properly, this can give you the downloads and reviews you need to gain enormous credibility and visibility on a global platform. Your eBook may even achieve a coveted "best seller" status as well!

But, there seems to be quite a bit of debate as to whether or not it's a beneficial way to market and sell your eBook, so I'm going to give you the facts and let you decide for yourself whether it's the right fit for you.

When you publish your eBook for sale on Amazon.com, you are also given the option of enrolling your eBook in the Kindle Select Program. By doing so, you are making your eBook available for Amazon Prime members to borrow it from the Kindle Owner's Lending Library. It's important to note however that you must offer your book for periods of 90 days at a time through the program, and you must re-enroll every 90 days if you choose to continue. What's in it for you? Enrolling in the program gives you the ability to allow all Amazon shoppers to get your eBook for FREE for 5 days with each 90-day enrollment period.

Sounds great doesn't it?

Well, not so fast. There are also some drawbacks I think you need to know about before you decide to take that step.

The downside, according to many self-published authors, is that once you enroll your eBook in the Kindle Select Program, you must remove it from selling on all other online retailer sites – including your own. This means you're selling your eBook EXCLUSIVELY on Amazon and nowhere else. This is where you need to get clear and make a decision as to the authentic purpose you have in self-publishing your eBook. If it's to sell books, then this may not be a good strategy for you in terms of achieving your goals.

BUT, if your true purpose is to use your eBook to attract more clients and build your business, then the Kindle Select Program is an awesome way to attract a lot more attention to your eBook and get the word out about your business.

The question you need to answer here is simple. Are you are promoting your BOOK, or are you promoting your BUSINESS?

And here's another big plus about enrolling your eBook in the program - under the Kindle Select Program's lending scheme, you get paid!

The amount of money you're paid, of course, depends on how many times your eBook is downloaded or borrowed, as well as the amount of money available in a lending fund Amazon has developed to entice more authors to offer their books through the program. It's important to note that any free downloads do not contribute to your sales rankings, but it will contribute to the number of reviews you receive and the buzz it will create, and hopefully to the number of people you are able to drive to your website.

For the entrepreneur author, your goal is to get your eBook into the hands of as many readers as possible, where they will learn about you, get to know, like, and trust you, and ultimately, make it over to your website to opt-in for that free gift you're offering. Your eBook is just a vehicle, and if you happen to make a few hundred dollars a month in sales, then that isn't so bad either, is it?

That's the real power behind eBooks – the ability to drive people to your website and get them to opt-in to your subscriber list. So, make use of Amazon's 5 free days with the Kindle Select Program, but plan this out carefully.

With this strategy, you have the ability to significantly increase your list size every 90 days simply by giving away your eBook every 90 days. This will then give you the ability to attract new clients and build their trust in you. Take that opportunity to engage with all the new members of your community by setting up and sending a series of auto responder emails and your eZine or newsletter. Having the ability to grow your list on demand in this way provides a strategic advantage and a golden opportunity for planning your promotions around these free day events, too. These are your list building bonus times, so work them all you can.

Learn From the Masters

As you embark on your grand eBook authoring and self-publishing adventure, I want you to study what other eBook authors have done.

Study the best-seller lists for the categories your eBook would best fit into on Amazon or B&N, taking careful note of which titles are selling best and which are not.

Carefully study the most downloaded free book. Which titles are being downloaded more than all the others? Study the eBook cover images of the most popular books. Study their titles, their book descriptions, and pricing. Read the first few pages or the "Look Inside" content. Buy the book, read it, and study the author's writing style and the structure of their book.

Read the customer reviews. What do people love or criticize about the book and what can you improve on?

Visit the author's website or blog and check out their profile on Author Central.

How are they marketing their book, or are they? What are they doing that you can model and what are they not doing that you can do? Analyze and dissect everything about these authors and learn from them.

Unlike the old world of traditional publishing where a book went to print and became a static, unchangeable object, your eBook is alive, and fluid, and dynamic!

This is your REAL opportunity. You can evolve it. You can change the cover image, the title, the price, the description, and you can even revise or update the book's content whenever you like. You can fine-tune the book until it connects with and resonates with as many readers as possible. Listen to your fans and strive to serve them.

CHAPTER 12

THE NEXT CHAPTER: WHY YOUR EBOOK IS YOUR NEW SECRET WEAPON FOR BUILDING A WILDLY PROFITABLE BUSINESS

-12-

*E*ntrepreneur Authors have a unique opportunity to leverage and re-purpose everything they create, whether it's a blog post, an interview, a newsletter article, or…an eBook. There are multiple revenue streams than can be generated out of the same content or processes you have already packaged into your eBook, adding a whole new dimension to the value your eBook can create.

Here are just a few ideas on how you can easily re-purpose and re-package the content from your eBook into multiple streams of income and the estimated fees you could potentially charge for each. I've also included a few passive income-generating opportunities as well.

- Audio books & MP3s: $5 - $100

- Workbooks: $50 - $100

- White papers and special reports: $50 - $100

- Info-products and home study programs: $100 - $3,000

- Tele-seminars: $200 - $1,500

- Boot camps and workshops: $200 - $2,500

- Video training: $200 - $2,500

- eCourses: $200 - $3,000

- Retreats: $500 - $5,000

- High-ticket VIP days and coaching programs: $3,000 – $10,000

- Memberships: $100 – $1,000 per month

As you can see, there is quite a range in potential revenue opportunities for each income stream. There are a number of key elements to consider when determining the pricing structure of your product or program such as length of time of the program, how the content is being delivered, the frequency of calls or meetings, level of access to the expert or trainer, and depth of the content being delivered.

Higher fees can be charged in service models where content is provided in a very short amount of time and in a private, exclusive setting. This makes full day VIP days and 1-on-1 coaching programs the must lucrative and profitable of all income streams to consider. Clients tend to pay more with less reluctance when they are able to obtain the information or training in a condensed period of time and when the content is delivered in a more private and exclusive format, where the trainer is focused completely on the client.

The key advantage to creating any of these products or programs, especially the high-ticket, VIP programs is that they add to the overall credibility of your business and enable you to position yourself as an expert in your area of expertise.

CLOSING THOUGHTS....

Without creating a whole new chapter, I want to leave you with a few quick tips and ideas. Here are some EASY things your can do today to prepare yourself for creating your own list building, lead generating eBook:

Sit down and do a download of everything you know about the topic you've chosen. Even if you don't use all the notes you come up with, you'll be able to use them for something else in the future like blog posts, articles, social media posts, or even your next eBook!

Go to Amazon.com and check out your competition for your book idea:

- What keywords and categories look good?
- What eCover elements are attractive?
- Check out the "Look Inside" feature.
- What bonuses can you offer?

Sign up for a good email management system that will allow you to easily create an opt-in form for your website where visitors can leave you with their name and email address. Some good ones to check out are AWeber, Constant Contact, and Mail Chimp.

Set up social networks. Build interesting and informative profiles on Face Book, Linked In, Google+, and Pinterest, and consistently be active on these platforms.

Hang out in forums where your ideal client or target reader is likely to be and ask questions about the members' biggest challenges and concerns.

Write an interesting bio to keep on hand and ready at a moment's notice. It's not only a critical credibility-booster to include in your eBook, but it can also be a credibility-killer if you happen to catch the attention of an event planner who is looking for a speaker at their next event and you have to take the time to quickly pull one together.

Lastly, go to www.robbinsimons.com/gurusecrets and download all the valuable cheat sheets and materials mentioned throughout this eBook. I want you to enjoy the process of creating and self-publishing your eBook, and these tools I've created for you are sure to make this process less stressful and a whole lot easier.

The VERY LAST thing I want to let you know about (I really mean it this time) is that I've created a SECRET Bonus Chapter. I came up with this chapter after the content for this eBook was already completed. My editing and formatting friends would have killed me if I asked them to revise the final version again, but I really wanted you to have this information, so I created a "stand-alone" chapter called *"7 GAME CHANGING Elements of a LEAD-GEN eBook"* and you can get this SECRET Bonus Chapter here:

www.SecretsTheGurusDontTeachYou.com

RESOURCES [BONUS SECTION]

Complimentary downloads, forms, and templates mentioned in this eBook are available for instant download at www.robbinsimons.com/gurusecrets.

For information about creating eBooks for attracting more clients, growing your subscriber list, and growing your business, go to www.robbinsimons.com or www.entrepreneurauthorelite.com

Need help creating your own client attracting, lead generating eBook? Here are a few resources I recommend:

Entrepreneur Author eBook Creation Program

www.entrepreneurauthorelite.com

Social Media Management

www.rebeccawardlow.com

The Story Stylist

www.storystylist.com

File Conversion Services

www.fileconversions.com

www.bibliotechbooks.com

IN GRATITUDE...

Thank you for downloading *eBook Publishing POWER for Entrepreneurs: SECRETS the Gurus Don't Teach You.*

I hope you found the content in this eBook helpful as you continue along your authoring or entrepreneurial journey.

I would be so grateful if you could take a minute or two and provide an honest review for this eBook on my Amazon sales page at:

http://www.amazon.com/Robbin-Simons/e/B00AR0IQSG/ref=sr_ntt_srch_lnk_1?qid=1375758187&sr=1-1

Wishing you inspiration & success,

Robbin

ONE LAST THING...

When you turn the page, Amazon will give you the opportunity to rate my eBook and share your experience and thoughts on Face Book and Twitter. If you believe this eBook is worth sharing, would you please take a few moments to let your friends know about it?

If it ends up helping Amazon sell more Kindle eBooks, they'll be equally as grateful to you as I will be.

http://www.amazon.com/Robbin-Simons/e/B00AR0IQSG/ref=sr_ntt_srch_lnk_1?qid=1375758187&sr=1-1

A WORD ABOUT COMMUNITY AND FRIENDSHIPS:

Community is something very special, and I'm always touched when members of my own community – my friends – step up to lend a hand, too. These very special and generous people, who I'm privileged to know, have all contributed a ton of bonus gifts to help you be better every day.

These gifts are exclusively available only to readers of this eBook, and include audios, videos, free coaching sessions, magazine subscriptions, and all kinds of other very cool training materials and tools from leading experts in the areas of health, wealth, and happiness.

You can grab all of these free gifts from my expert friends here:

www.secretsthegurusdontteachyou.com

FINALLY....

I've created a couple of special social media groups where entrepreneur authors from all niches and locations around the world can meet, interact, and share ideas.

If Face Book is your thing, then visit me on my fan page at:

www.facebook.com/robbinsimonsfans

If you're more of a Linked In type of person, come & join my group called *"Publish, Promote, Prosper"* at:

www.linkedin.com/groups/Publish-Promote-Prosper

More Kindle eBooks by Robbin:

The Holistic Health & Wellness Entrepreneur's Essential Handbook for Success: Make More Money Doing What You Love

Available exclusively from Amazon.com

ABOUT THE AUTHOR
ROBBIN SIMONS

My Official Bio....

Robbin Simons is the leading expert on lead generation eBook publishing and sales conversion for entrepreneur authors. She is a speaker, author, and "go-to" mentor for entrepreneurs seeking to establish expert credibility, build their subscriber lists, and gain global visibility by creating their own lead generation eBook. In her unique Entrepreneur Author programs, Robbin helps her clients leverage existing content to quickly and easily create and self-publish an eBook structured specifically for list building and lead generation, resulting in the potential to generate 1000's of qualified new leads each month, without ever spending a dime on advertising.

You can learn more about Robbin and all of her Entrepreneur Author programs and download your complimentary *EASY eBook Creation Toolkit* at: www.robbinsimons.com/starthere/

And here's a little more about me…

Over the past 20 years, I have enjoyed a very successful corporate career in field of Supply Chain working with global Fortune 500 companies in the information technology, retail, and life sciences industries. I have even been fortunate enough to be recognized by Supply & Demand Chain Executive as a **"2011 Practitioner Pro to Know"**. But with all of this, I still felt the desire to do something more meaningful with my life…something more authentic where I could truly make a difference in peoples' lives.

I began my journey by re-connecting with my own energies and purpose, spending many years studying and practicing various Holistic Therapies, including Iridology, Reiki, Holistic Nutrition, and others.

Using my previous corporate background and skills, I started my entrepreneurial journey with my own Holistic Therapy business. I did all the things entrepreneurs do to market their businesses. I tried Facebook ads, Google Ad Words, etc. but I wasn't getting a decent ROI (return on investment) so I started looking for other alternatives.

That's when I found an eBook on the subject of online marketing. But it wasn't so much the content of the eBook that I found intriguing. It was the structure of the eBook itself that I became fascinated with. As I began to investigate the technology behind the eBook format, I clearly saw an opportunity to write and structure eBooks in a way that entrepreneurs and authors could use them as a tool to generate qualified leads and attract more ideal clients.

From that point forward, my business model and purpose changed. I saw that many entrepreneurs were missing out on greater opportunities to use a book, content, or information they had already created to attract more clients and get their message out into the world in a bigger way.

Author of *The Holistic Health & Wellness Entrepreneur's Essential Handbook for Success:*

Easy Ways to Make More Money Doing What You Love, available at www.amazon.com

Publisher of the bi-weekly online eZine *"Hot Off the Press"*: a publication for all Emerging Entrepreneurs who are seeking easy-to-implement guidance, tips, and support as they launch and grow their heart-centered businesses using the HOTTEST and COOLEST media options available today.

Contributing Expert for *Today's Innovative Woman Magazine*: An online and print magazine dedicated to entrepreneur women. From women just launching a business to veteran entrepreneurs, Today's Innovative Woman Magazine offers a wealth of information from A to Z.

Contributing Expert for *Life.Business.Growth*: an online community of conscious women entrepreneurs, created to provide education, connection and inspiration to other women entrepreneurs.

Contributing Expert for *Business Heroine Magazine*: an online magazine designed to inspire the feminine leader and honor the women in business who said they would and did. It is their mission is to help women unlock their unique genius so they can build a designer brand around their talents and ultimately create financial freedom.

eBook Publishing POWER for Entrepreneurs: SECRETS the Gurus Don't Teach You

Robbin Simons

Crescendo Publishing LLC

www.crescendopublishing.com

Published by Crescendo Publishing LLC

Suite 108A, #443,

300 Carlsbad Village Drive

Carlsbad, California 92008-2999

Copyright 2013 by Robbin Simons

All Rights Reserved. No part of this publication may not ne reproduced, transmitted, downloaded in whole or in part in any form without the express written consent of the Publisher. Reviewers May quote brief passages in reviews.

Neither the author nor the publisher assumes any responsibility or liability whatsoever on behalf of the reader or the purchaser of these materials.

This book is for entertainment purposes only. The views expressed are those of the author alone, and should not be taken as expert instruction or commands. The reader is responsible for his or her own actions.

www.robbinsimons.com

www.CrescendoPublishing.com

ROBBIN SIMONS

LEGAL DISCLAIMER:

Every effort has been made to accurately represent this material and its potential. Any claims made of actual results can be verified upon request. The testimonials and examples used are exceptional results, don't apply to the average purchaser, and are not intended to guarantee anyone will achieve the same or similar results. Each individual's success depends on his or her background and commitment.

ROBBIN SIMONS

www.ingramcontent.com/pod-product-compliance
Lightning Source LLC
Chambersburg PA
CBHW051524170526
45165CB00002B/596